Log Book Detai

Log Start Date:	
Log Book Number:	

Details

Company / Name:	
Registration Details:	
Address:	
Phone Number:	
Fax Number:	
Email Address:	

Date		Description	Reference	Debit	Credit
/ /					
/ /					
/ /					
/ /					
/ /					
/ /					
/ /					
/ /					
/ /					
/ /					
/ /					
/ /					
/ /					
/ /					
/ /					
/ /					
/ /					
/ /					
/ /					
/ /					
/ /					
/ /					

Date	Description	Reference	Debit	Credit
/ /				
/ /				
/ /				
/ /				
/ /				
/ /				
/ /				
/ /				
/ /				
/ /				
/ /				
/ /				
/ /				
/ /				
/ /				
/ /				
/ /				
/ /				
/ /				
/ /				
/ /				
/ /				
/ /				

Date		Description	Reference	Debit	Credit
/ /					
/ /					
/ /					
/ /					
/ /					
/ /					
/ /					
/ /					
/ /					
/ /					
/ /					
/ /					
/ /					
/ /					
/ /					
/ /					
/ /					
/ /					
/ /					
/ /					
/ /					
/ /					
/ /					

Date	Description	Reference	Debit	Credit
/ /				
/ /				
/ /				
/ /				
/ /				
/ /				
/ /				
/ /				
/ /				
/ /				
/ /				
/ /				
/ /				
/ /				
/ /				
/ /				
/ /				
/ /				
/ /				
/ /				
/ /				
/ /				

Date		Description	Reference	Debit	Credit
/ /					
/ /					
/ /					
/ /					
/ /					
/ /					
/ /					
/ /					
/ /					
/ /					
/ /					
/ /					
/ /					
/ /					
/ /					
/ /					
/ /					
/ /					
/ /					
/ /					
/ /					
/ /					
/ /					

Date		Description	Reference	Debit	Credit
/ /					
/ /					
/ /					
/ /					
/ /					
/ /					
/ /					
/ /					
/ /					
/ /					
/ /					
/ /					
/ /					
/ /					
/ /					
/ /					
/ /					
/ /					
/ /					
/ /					
/ /					
/ /					
/ /					

Date		Description	Reference	Debit	Credit
/ /					
/ /					
/ /					
/ /					
/ /					
/ /					
/ /					
/ /					
/ /					
/ /					
/ /					
/ /					
/ /					
/ /					
/ /					
/ /					
/ /					
/ /					
/ /					
/ /					
/ /					
/ /					

Date		Description	Reference	Debit	Credit
/ /					
/ /					
/ /					
/ /					
/ /					
/ /					
/ /					
/ /					
/ /					
/ /					
/ /					
/ /					
/ /					
/ /					
/ /					
/ /					
/ /					
/ /					
/ /					
/ /					
/ /					
/ /					

Date	Description	Reference	Debit	Credit
/ /				
/ /				
/ /				
/ /				
/ /				
/ /				
/ /				
/ /				
/ /				
/ /				
/ /				
/ /				
/ /				
/ /				
/ /				
/ /				
/ /				
/ /				
/ /				
/ /				
/ /				
/ /				
/ /				

Date	Description	Reference	Debit	Credit
/ /				
/ /				
/ /				
/ /				
/ /				
/ /				
/ /				
/ /				
/ /				
/ /				
/ /				
/ /				
/ /				
/ /				
/ /				
/ /				
/ /				
/ /				
/ /				
/ /				
/ /				
/ /				
/ /				

Date		Description	Reference	Debit	Credit
/ /					
/ /					
/ /					
/ /					
/ /					
/ /					
/ /					
/ /					
/ /					
/ /					
/ /					
/ /					
/ /					
/ /					
/ /					
/ /					
/ /					
/ /					
/ /					
/ /					
/ /					
/ /					

Date		Description	Reference	Debit	Credit
/ /					
/ /					
/ /					
/ /					
/ /					
/ /					
/ /					
/ /					
/ /					
/ /					
/ /					
/ /					
/ /					
/ /					
/ /					
/ /					
/ /					
/ /					
/ /					
/ /					
/ /					
/ /					

Date		Description	Reference	Debit	Credit
/ /					
/ /					
/ /					
/ /					
/ /					
/ /					
/ /					
/ /					
/ /					
/ /					
/ /					
/ /					
/ /					
/ /					
/ /					
/ /					
/ /					
/ /					
/ /					
/ /					
/ /					
/ /					
/ /					
/ /					

Date	Description	Reference	Debit	Credit
/ /				
/ /				
/ /				
/ /				
/ /				
/ /				
/ /				
/ /				
/ /				
/ /				
/ /				
/ /				
/ /				
/ /				
/ /				
/ /				
/ /				
/ /				
/ /				
/ /				
/ /				
/ /				
/ /				

Date		Description	Reference	Debit	Credit
/ /					
/ /					
/ /					
/ /					
/ /					
/ /					
/ /					
/ /					
/ /					
/ /					
/ /					
/ /					
/ /					
/ /					
/ /					
/ /					
/ /					
/ /					
/ /					
/ /					
/ /					
/ /					

Date		Description	Reference	Debit	Credit
/ /					
/ /					
/ /					
/ /					
/ /					
/ /					
/ /					
/ /					
/ /					
/ /					
/ /					
/ /					
/ /					
/ /					
/ /					
/ /					
/ /					
/ /					
/ /					
/ /					
/ /					
/ /					
/ /					

Date		Description	Reference	Debit	Credit
/ /					
/ /					
/ /					
/ /					
/ /					
/ /					
/ /					
/ /					
/ /					
/ /					
/ /					
/ /					
/ /					
/ /					
/ /					
/ /					
/ /					
/ /					
/ /					
/ /					
/ /					
/ /					
/ /					

Date		Description	Reference	Debit	Credit
/ /					
/ /					
/ /					
/ /					
/ /					
/ /					
/ /					
/ /					
/ /					
/ /					
/ /					
/ /					
/ /					
/ /					
/ /					
/ /					
/ /					
/ /					
/ /					
/ /					
/ /					
/ /					
/ /					

Date		Description	Reference	Debit	Credit
/ /					
/ /					
/ /					
/ /					
/ /					
/ /					
/ /					
/ /					
/ /					
/ /					
/ /					
/ /					
/ /					
/ /					
/ /					
/ /					
/ /					
/ /					
/ /					
/ /					
/ /					
/ /					

Date		Description	Reference	Debit	Credit
/ /					
/ /					
/ /					
/ /					
/ /					
/ /					
/ /					
/ /					
/ /					
/ /					
/ /					
/ /					
/ /					
/ /					
/ /					
/ /					
/ /					
/ /					
/ /					
/ /					
/ /					
/ /					

Date		Description	Reference	Debit	Credit
/ /					
/ /					
/ /					
/ /					
/ /					
/ /					
/ /					
/ /					
/ /					
/ /					
/ /					
/ /					
/ /					
/ /					
/ /					
/ /					
/ /					
/ /					
/ /					
/ /					
/ /					
/ /					

Date	Description	Reference	Debit	Credit
/ /				
/ /				
/ /				
/ /				
/ /				
/ /				
/ /				
/ /				
/ /				
/ /				
/ /				
/ /				
/ /				
/ /				
/ /				
/ /				
/ /				
/ /				
/ /				
/ /				
/ /				
/ /				

Date		Description	Reference	Debit	Credit
/ /					
/ /					
/ /					
/ /					
/ /					
/ /					
/ /					
/ /					
/ /					
/ /					
/ /					
/ /					
/ /					
/ /					
/ /					
/ /					
/ /					
/ /					
/ /					
/ /					
/ /					
/ /					

Date		Description	Reference	Debit	Credit
/ /					
/ /					
/ /					
/ /					
/ /					
/ /					
/ /					
/ /					
/ /					
/ /					
/ /					
/ /					
/ /					
/ /					
/ /					
/ /					
/ /					
/ /					
/ /					
/ /					
/ /					
/ /					
/ /					

Date		Description	Reference	Debit	Credit
/ /					
/ /					
/ /					
/ /					
/ /					
/ /					
/ /					
/ /					
/ /					
/ /					
/ /					
/ /					
/ /					
/ /					
/ /					
/ /					
/ /					
/ /					
/ /					
/ /					
/ /					
/ /					
/ /					

Date		Description	Reference	Debit	Credit
/ /					
/ /					
/ /					
/ /					
/ /					
/ /					
/ /					
/ /					
/ /					
/ /					
/ /					
/ /					
/ /					
/ /					
/ /					
/ /					
/ /					
/ /					
/ /					
/ /					
/ /					
/ /					

Date		Description	Reference	Debit	Credit
/ /					
/ /					
/ /					
/ /					
/ /					
/ /					
/ /					
/ /					
/ /					
/ /					
/ /					
/ /					
/ /					
/ /					
/ /					
/ /					
/ /					
/ /					
/ /					
/ /					
/ /					
/ /					

Date	Description	Reference	Debit	Credit
/ /				
/ /				
/ /				
/ /				
/ /				
/ /				
/ /				
/ /				
/ /				
/ /				
/ /				
/ /				
/ /				
/ /				
/ /				
/ /				
/ /				
/ /				
/ /				
/ /				
/ /				
/ /				
/ /				

Date		Description	Reference	Debit	Credit
/ /					
/ /					
/ /					
/ /					
/ /					
/ /					
/ /					
/ /					
/ /					
/ /					
/ /					
/ /					
/ /					
/ /					
/ /					
/ /					
/ /					
/ /					
/ /					
/ /					
/ /					
/ /					

Date		Description	Reference	Debit	Credit
/ /					
/ /					
/ /					
/ /					
/ /					
/ /					
/ /					
/ /					
/ /					
/ /					
/ /					
/ /					
/ /					
/ /					
/ /					
/ /					
/ /					
/ /					
/ /					
/ /					
/ /					
/ /					

Date		Description	Reference	Debit	Credit
/ /					
/ /					
/ /					
/ /					
/ /					
/ /					
/ /					
/ /					
/ /					
/ /					
/ /					
/ /					
/ /					
/ /					
/ /					
/ /					
/ /					
/ /					
/ /					
/ /					
/ /					
/ /					
/ /					

Date		Description	Reference	Debit	Credit
/ /					
/ /					
/ /					
/ /					
/ /					
/ /					
/ /					
/ /					
/ /					
/ /					
/ /					
/ /					
/ /					
/ /					
/ /					
/ /					
/ /					
/ /					
/ /					
/ /					
/ /					
/ /					
/ /					

Date		Description	Reference	Debit	Credit
/ /					
/ /					
/ /					
/ /					
/ /					
/ /					
/ /					
/ /					
/ /					
/ /					
/ /					
/ /					
/ /					
/ /					
/ /					
/ /					
/ /					
/ /					
/ /					
/ /					
/ /					
/ /					
/ /					

Date	Description	Reference	Debit	Credit
/ /				
/ /				
/ /				
/ /				
/ /				
/ /				
/ /				
/ /				
/ /				
/ /				
/ /				
/ /				
/ /				
/ /				
/ /				
/ /				
/ /				
/ /				
/ /				
/ /				
/ /				
/ /				
/ /				
/ /				

Date		Description	Reference	Debit	Credit
/ /					
/ /					
/ /					
/ /					
/ /					
/ /					
/ /					
/ /					
/ /					
/ /					
/ /					
/ /					
/ /					
/ /					
/ /					
/ /					
/ /					
/ /					
/ /					
/ /					
/ /					
/ /					

Date		Description	Reference	Debit	Credit
/ /					
/ /					
/ /					
/ /					
/ /					
/ /					
/ /					
/ /					
/ /					
/ /					
/ /					
/ /					
/ /					
/ /					
/ /					
/ /					
/ /					
/ /					
/ /					
/ /					
/ /					
/ /					

Date	Description	Reference	Debit	Credit
/ /				
/ /				
/ /				
/ /				
/ /				
/ /				
/ /				
/ /				
/ /				
/ /				
/ /				
/ /				
/ /				
/ /				
/ /				
/ /				
/ /				
/ /				
/ /				
/ /				
/ /				
/ /				

Date		Description	Reference	Debit	Credit
/ /					
/ /					
/ /					
/ /					
/ /					
/ /					
/ /					
/ /					
/ /					
/ /					
/ /					
/ /					
/ /					
/ /					
/ /					
/ /					
/ /					
/ /					
/ /					
/ /					
/ /					
/ /					

Date		Description	Reference	Debit	Credit
/ /					
/ /					
/ /					
/ /					
/ /					
/ /					
/ /					
/ /					
/ /					
/ /					
/ /					
/ /					
/ /					
/ /					
/ /					
/ /					
/ /					
/ /					
/ /					
/ /					
/ /					
/ /					
/ /					

Date		Description	Reference	Debit	Credit
/ /					
/ /					
/ /					
/ /					
/ /					
/ /					
/ /					
/ /					
/ /					
/ /					
/ /					
/ /					
/ /					
/ /					
/ /					
/ /					
/ /					
/ /					
/ /					
/ /					
/ /					
/ /					

Date		Description	Reference	Debit	Credit
/ /					
/ /					
/ /					
/ /					
/ /					
/ /					
/ /					
/ /					
/ /					
/ /					
/ /					
/ /					
/ /					
/ /					
/ /					
/ /					
/ /					
/ /					
/ /					
/ /					
/ /					
/ /					
/ /					
/ /					

Date		Description	Reference	Debit	Credit
/ /					
/ /					
/ /					
/ /					
/ /					
/ /					
/ /					
/ /					
/ /					
/ /					
/ /					
/ /					
/ /					
/ /					
/ /					
/ /					
/ /					
/ /					
/ /					
/ /					
/ /					
/ /					

Date		Description	Reference	Debit	Credit
/ /					
/ /					
/ /					
/ /					
/ /					
/ /					
/ /					
/ /					
/ /					
/ /					
/ /					
/ /					
/ /					
/ /					
/ /					
/ /					
/ /					
/ /					
/ /					
/ /					
/ /					
/ /					
/ /					

Date		Description	Reference	Debit	Credit
/ /					
/ /					
/ /					
/ /					
/ /					
/ /					
/ /					
/ /					
/ /					
/ /					
/ /					
/ /					
/ /					
/ /					
/ /					
/ /					
/ /					
/ /					
/ /					
/ /					
/ /					
/ /					

Date		Description	Reference	Debit	Credit
/ /					
/ /					
/ /					
/ /					
/ /					
/ /					
/ /					
/ /					
/ /					
/ /					
/ /					
/ /					
/ /					
/ /					
/ /					
/ /					
/ /					
/ /					
/ /					
/ /					
/ /					
/ /					

Date		Description	Reference	Debit	Credit
/ /					
/ /					
/ /					
/ /					
/ /					
/ /					
/ /					
/ /					
/ /					
/ /					
/ /					
/ /					
/ /					
/ /					
/ /					
/ /					
/ /					
/ /					
/ /					
/ /					
/ /					
/ /					
/ /					

Date		Description	Reference	Debit	Credit
/ /					
/ /					
/ /					
/ /					
/ /					
/ /					
/ /					
/ /					
/ /					
/ /					
/ /					
/ /					
/ /					
/ /					
/ /					
/ /					
/ /					
/ /					
/ /					
/ /					
/ /					
/ /					
/ /					

Date	Description	Reference	Debit	Credit
/ /				
/ /				
/ /				
/ /				
/ /				
/ /				
/ /				
/ /				
/ /				
/ /				
/ /				
/ /				
/ /				
/ /				
/ /				
/ /				
/ /				
/ /				
/ /				
/ /				
/ /				
/ /				
/ /				

Date		Description	Reference	Debit	Credit
/ /					
/ /					
/ /					
/ /					
/ /					
/ /					
/ /					
/ /					
/ /					
/ /					
/ /					
/ /					
/ /					
/ /					
/ /					
/ /					
/ /					
/ /					
/ /					
/ /					
/ /					
/ /					
/ /					

Date	Description	Reference	Debit	Credit
/ /				
/ /				
/ /				
/ /				
/ /				
/ /				
/ /				
/ /				
/ /				
/ /				
/ /				
/ /				
/ /				
/ /				
/ /				
/ /				
/ /				
/ /				
/ /				
/ /				
/ /				
/ /				
/ /				

Date	Description	Reference	Debit	Credit
/ /				
/ /				
/ /				
/ /				
/ /				
/ /				
/ /				
/ /				
/ /				
/ /				
/ /				
/ /				
/ /				
/ /				
/ /				
/ /				
/ /				
/ /				
/ /				
/ /				
/ /				
/ /				

Date	Description	Reference	Debit	Credit
/ /				
/ /				
/ /				
/ /				
/ /				
/ /				
/ /				
/ /				
/ /				
/ /				
/ /				
/ /				
/ /				
/ /				
/ /				
/ /				
/ /				
/ /				
/ /				
/ /				
/ /				
/ /				
/ /				

Date		Description	Reference	Debit	Credit
/ /					
/ /					
/ /					
/ /					
/ /					
/ /					
/ /					
/ /					
/ /					
/ /					
/ /					
/ /					
/ /					
/ /					
/ /					
/ /					
/ /					
/ /					
/ /					
/ /					
/ /					
/ /					

Date	Description	Reference	Debit	Credit
/ /				
/ /				
/ /				
/ /				
/ /				
/ /				
/ /				
/ /				
/ /				
/ /				
/ /				
/ /				
/ /				
/ /				
/ /				
/ /				
/ /				
/ /				
/ /				
/ /				
/ /				
/ /				
/ /				
/ /				

Date	Description	Reference	Debit	Credit
/ /				
/ /				
/ /				
/ /				
/ /				
/ /				
/ /				
/ /				
/ /				
/ /				
/ /				
/ /				
/ /				
/ /				
/ /				
/ /				
/ /				
/ /				
/ /				
/ /				
/ /				
/ /				
/ /				

Date	Description	Reference	Debit	Credit
/ /				
/ /				
/ /				
/ /				
/ /				
/ /				
/ /				
/ /				
/ /				
/ /				
/ /				
/ /				
/ /				
/ /				
/ /				
/ /				
/ /				
/ /				
/ /				
/ /				
/ /				
/ /				
/ /				

Date	Description	Reference	Debit	Credit
/ /				
/ /				
/ /				
/ /				
/ /				
/ /				
/ /				
/ /				
/ /				
/ /				
/ /				
/ /				
/ /				
/ /				
/ /				
/ /				
/ /				
/ /				
/ /				
/ /				
/ /				
/ /				
/ /				

Date	Description	Reference	Debit	Credit
/ /				
/ /				
/ /				
/ /				
/ /				
/ /				
/ /				
/ /				
/ /				
/ /				
/ /				
/ /				
/ /				
/ /				
/ /				
/ /				
/ /				
/ /				
/ /				
/ /				
/ /				
/ /				
/ /				

Date		Description	Reference	Debit	Credit
/ /					
/ /					
/ /					
/ /					
/ /					
/ /					
/ /					
/ /					
/ /					
/ /					
/ /					
/ /					
/ /					
/ /					
/ /					
/ /					
/ /					
/ /					
/ /					
/ /					
/ /					
/ /					

Date		Description	Reference	Debit	Credit
/ /					
/ /					
/ /					
/ /					
/ /					
/ /					
/ /					
/ /					
/ /					
/ /					
/ /					
/ /					
/ /					
/ /					
/ /					
/ /					
/ /					
/ /					
/ /					
/ /					
/ /					
/ /					

Date		Description	Reference	Debit	Credit
/ /					
/ /					
/ /					
/ /					
/ /					
/ /					
/ /					
/ /					
/ /					
/ /					
/ /					
/ /					
/ /					
/ /					
/ /					
/ /					
/ /					
/ /					
/ /					
/ /					
/ /					
/ /					

Date	Description	Reference	Debit	Credit
/ /				
/ /				
/ /				
/ /				
/ /				
/ /				
/ /				
/ /				
/ /				
/ /				
/ /				
/ /				
/ /				
/ /				
/ /				
/ /				
/ /				
/ /				
/ /				
/ /				
/ /				
/ /				
/ /				

Date		Description	Reference	Debit	Credit
/ /					
/ /					
/ /					
/ /					
/ /					
/ /					
/ /					
/ /					
/ /					
/ /					
/ /					
/ /					
/ /					
/ /					
/ /					
/ /					
/ /					
/ /					
/ /					
/ /					
/ /					

Date	Description	Reference	Debit	Credit
/ /				
/ /				
/ /				
/ /				
/ /				
/ /				
/ /				
/ /				
/ /				
/ /				
/ /				
/ /				
/ /				
/ /				
/ /				
/ /				
/ /				
/ /				
/ /				
/ /				
/ /				
/ /				

Date		Description	Reference	Debit	Credit
/ /					
/ /					
/ /					
/ /					
/ /					
/ /					
/ /					
/ /					
/ /					
/ /					
/ /					
/ /					
/ /					
/ /					
/ /					
/ /					
/ /					
/ /					
/ /					
/ /					
/ /					
/ /					

Date		Description	Reference	Debit	Credit
/ /					
/ /					
/ /					
/ /					
/ /					
/ /					
/ /					
/ /					
/ /					
/ /					
/ /					
/ /					
/ /					
/ /					
/ /					
/ /					
/ /					
/ /					
/ /					
/ /					
/ /					
/ /					

Date	Description	Reference	Debit	Credit
/ /				
/ /				
/ /				
/ /				
/ /				
/ /				
/ /				
/ /				
/ /				
/ /				
/ /				
/ /				
/ /				
/ /				
/ /				
/ /				
/ /				
/ /				
/ /				
/ /				
/ /				
/ /				
/ /				

Date		Description	Reference	Debit	Credit
/ /					
/ /					
/ /					
/ /					
/ /					
/ /					
/ /					
/ /					
/ /					
/ /					
/ /					
/ /					
/ /					
/ /					
/ /					
/ /					
/ /					
/ /					
/ /					
/ /					
/ /					
/ /					
/ /					

Date		Description	Reference	Debit	Credit
/ /					
/ /					
/ /					
/ /					
/ /					
/ /					
/ /					
/ /					
/ /					
/ /					
/ /					
/ /					
/ /					
/ /					
/ /					
/ /					
/ /					
/ /					
/ /					
/ /					
/ /					
/ /					
/ /					

Date		Description	Reference	Debit	Credit
/ /					
/ /					
/ /					
/ /					
/ /					
/ /					
/ /					
/ /					
/ /					
/ /					
/ /					
/ /					
/ /					
/ /					
/ /					
/ /					
/ /					
/ /					
/ /					
/ /					
/ /					
/ /					

Date		Description	Reference	Debit	Credit
/ /					
/ /					
/ /					
/ /					
/ /					
/ /					
/ /					
/ /					
/ /					
/ /					
/ /					
/ /					
/ /					
/ /					
/ /					
/ /					
/ /					
/ /					
/ /					
/ /					
/ /					
/ /					

Date		Description	Reference	Debit	Credit
/ /					
/ /					
/ /					
/ /					
/ /					
/ /					
/ /					
/ /					
/ /					
/ /					
/ /					
/ /					
/ /					
/ /					
/ /					
/ /					
/ /					
/ /					
/ /					
/ /					
/ /					
/ /					

Date		Description	Reference	Debit	Credit
/ /					
/ /					
/ /					
/ /					
/ /					
/ /					
/ /					
/ /					
/ /					
/ /					
/ /					
/ /					
/ /					
/ /					
/ /					
/ /					
/ /					
/ /					
/ /					
/ /					
/ /					
/ /					
/ /					

Date	Description	Reference	Debit	Credit
/ /				
/ /				
/ /				
/ /				
/ /				
/ /				
/ /				
/ /				
/ /				
/ /				
/ /				
/ /				
/ /				
/ /				
/ /				
/ /				
/ /				
/ /				
/ /				
/ /				
/ /				
/ /				

Date		Description	Reference	Debit	Credit
/ /					
/ /					
/ /					
/ /					
/ /					
/ /					
/ /					
/ /					
/ /					
/ /					
/ /					
/ /					
/ /					
/ /					
/ /					
/ /					
/ /					
/ /					
/ /					
/ /					
/ /					
/ /					
/ /					

Date		Description	Reference	Debit	Credit
/ /					
/ /					
/ /					
/ /					
/ /					
/ /					
/ /					
/ /					
/ /					
/ /					
/ /					
/ /					
/ /					
/ /					
/ /					
/ /					
/ /					
/ /					
/ /					
/ /					
/ /					
/ /					
/ /					

Date		Description	Reference	Debit	Credit
/ /					
/ /					
/ /					
/ /					
/ /					
/ /					
/ /					
/ /					
/ /					
/ /					
/ /					
/ /					
/ /					
/ /					
/ /					
/ /					
/ /					
/ /					
/ /					
/ /					
/ /					
/ /					

Date	Description	Reference	Debit	Credit
/ /				
/ /				
/ /				
/ /				
/ /				
/ /				
/ /				
/ /				
/ /				
/ /				
/ /				
/ /				
/ /				
/ /				
/ /				
/ /				
/ /				
/ /				
/ /				
/ /				
/ /				
/ /				

Date		Description	Reference	Debit	Credit
/ /					
/ /					
/ /					
/ /					
/ /					
/ /					
/ /					
/ /					
/ /					
/ /					
/ /					
/ /					
/ /					
/ /					
/ /					
/ /					
/ /					
/ /					
/ /					
/ /					
/ /					
/ /					

Date		Description	Reference	Debit	Credit
/ /					
/ /					
/ /					
/ /					
/ /					
/ /					
/ /					
/ /					
/ /					
/ /					
/ /					
/ /					
/ /					
/ /					
/ /					
/ /					
/ /					
/ /					
/ /					
/ /					
/ /					
/ /					

Date		Description	Reference	Debit	Credit
/ /					
/ /					
/ /					
/ /					
/ /					
/ /					
/ /					
/ /					
/ /					
/ /					
/ /					
/ /					
/ /					
/ /					
/ /					
/ /					
/ /					
/ /					
/ /					
/ /					
/ /					
/ /					
/ /					

Date	Description	Reference	Debit	Credit
/ /				
/ /				
/ /				
/ /				
/ /				
/ /				
/ /				
/ /				
/ /				
/ /				
/ /				
/ /				
/ /				
/ /				
/ /				
/ /				
/ /				
/ /				
/ /				
/ /				
/ /				
/ /				

Date		Description	Reference	Debit	Credit
/ /					
/ /					
/ /					
/ /					
/ /					
/ /					
/ /					
/ /					
/ /					
/ /					
/ /					
/ /					
/ /					
/ /					
/ /					
/ /					
/ /					
/ /					
/ /					
/ /					
/ /					
/ /					
/ /					

Date		Description	Reference	Debit	Credit
/ /					
/ /					
/ /					
/ /					
/ /					
/ /					
/ /					
/ /					
/ /					
/ /					
/ /					
/ /					
/ /					
/ /					
/ /					
/ /					
/ /					
/ /					
/ /					
/ /					
/ /					
/ /					

Date		Description	Reference	Debit	Credit
/ /					
/ /					
/ /					
/ /					
/ /					
/ /					
/ /					
/ /					
/ /					
/ /					
/ /					
/ /					
/ /					
/ /					
/ /					
/ /					
/ /					
/ /					
/ /					
/ /					
/ /					
/ /					

Date	Description	Reference	Debit	Credit
/ /				
/ /				
/ /				
/ /				
/ /				
/ /				
/ /				
/ /				
/ /				
/ /				
/ /				
/ /				
/ /				
/ /				
/ /				
/ /				
/ /				
/ /				
/ /				
/ /				
/ /				
/ /				
/ /				

Date		Description	Reference	Debit	Credit
/ /					
/ /					
/ /					
/ /					
/ /					
/ /					
/ /					
/ /					
/ /					
/ /					
/ /					
/ /					
/ /					
/ /					
/ /					
/ /					
/ /					
/ /					
/ /					
/ /					
/ /					
/ /					

Date		Description	Reference	Debit	Credit
/ /					
/ /					
/ /					
/ /					
/ /					
/ /					
/ /					
/ /					
/ /					
/ /					
/ /					
/ /					
/ /					
/ /					
/ /					
/ /					
/ /					
/ /					
/ /					
/ /					
/ /					
/ /					

Date		Description	Reference	Debit	Credit
/ /					
/ /					
/ /					
/ /					
/ /					
/ /					
/ /					
/ /					
/ /					
/ /					
/ /					
/ /					
/ /					
/ /					
/ /					
/ /					
/ /					
/ /					
/ /					
/ /					
/ /					
/ /					
/ /					

Date	Description	Reference	Debit	Credit
/ /				
/ /				
/ /				
/ /				
/ /				
/ /				
/ /				
/ /				
/ /				
/ /				
/ /				
/ /				
/ /				
/ /				
/ /				
/ /				
/ /				
/ /				
/ /				
/ /				
/ /				
/ /				
/ /				

Date		Description	Reference	Debit	Credit
/ /					
/ /					
/ /					
/ /					
/ /					
/ /					
/ /					
/ /					
/ /					
/ /					
/ /					
/ /					
/ /					
/ /					
/ /					
/ /					
/ /					
/ /					
/ /					
/ /					
/ /					
/ /					
/ /					

Date		Description	Reference	Debit	Credit
/ /					
/ /					
/ /					
/ /					
/ /					
/ /					
/ /					
/ /					
/ /					
/ /					
/ /					
/ /					
/ /					
/ /					
/ /					
/ /					
/ /					
/ /					
/ /					
/ /					
/ /					
/ /					
/ /					

Date	Description	Reference	Debit	Credit
/ /				
/ /				
/ /				
/ /				
/ /				
/ /				
/ /				
/ /				
/ /				
/ /				
/ /				
/ /				
/ /				
/ /				
/ /				
/ /				
/ /				
/ /				
/ /				
/ /				
/ /				
/ /				
/ /				

Date		Description	Reference	Debit	Credit
/ /					
/ /					
/ /					
/ /					
/ /					
/ /					
/ /					
/ /					
/ /					
/ /					
/ /					
/ /					
/ /					
/ /					
/ /					
/ /					
/ /					
/ /					
/ /					
/ /					
/ /					
/ /					
/ /					

Date		Description	Reference	Debit	Credit
/ /					
/ /					
/ /					
/ /					
/ /					
/ /					
/ /					
/ /					
/ /					
/ /					
/ /					
/ /					
/ /					
/ /					
/ /					
/ /					
/ /					
/ /					
/ /					
/ /					
/ /					
/ /					

Date		Description	Reference	Debit	Credit
/ /					
/ /					
/ /					
/ /					
/ /					
/ /					
/ /					
/ /					
/ /					
/ /					
/ /					
/ /					
/ /					
/ /					
/ /					
/ /					
/ /					
/ /					
/ /					
/ /					
/ /					
/ /					
/ /					

Date		Description	Reference	Debit	Credit
/ /					
/ /					
/ /					
/ /					
/ /					
/ /					
/ /					
/ /					
/ /					
/ /					
/ /					
/ /					
/ /					
/ /					
/ /					
/ /					
/ /					
/ /					
/ /					
/ /					
/ /					
/ /					

Date		Description	Reference	Debit	Credit
/ /					
/ /					
/ /					
/ /					
/ /					
/ /					
/ /					
/ /					
/ /					
/ /					
/ /					
/ /					
/ /					
/ /					
/ /					
/ /					
/ /					
/ /					
/ /					
/ /					
/ /					
/ /					

Made in the USA
Monee, IL
13 December 2023

49201603R00059